STEM IN SPORTS:
TECHNOLOGY

THE STEM IN SPORTS SERIES

STEM in Sports: Science, by Jim Gigliotti

STEM in Sports: Technology, by James Buckley, Jr.

STEM in Sports: Engineering, by Tim Newcomb

STEM in Sports: Math, by James Buckley Jr.

STEM IN SPORTS:
TECHNOLOGY

by James Buckley Jr.

SCIENCE   TECHNOLOGY   ENGINEERING   MATH

Mason Crest
450 Parkway Drive, Suite D
Broomall, PA 19008
www.masoncrest.com

Printed and bound in the United States of America.

Series ISBN: 978-1-4222-3230-9
Hardback ISBN: 978-1-4222-3234-7
EBook ISBN: 978-1-4222-8678-4

First printing
1 3 5 7 9 8 6 4 2

Produced by Shoreline Publishing Group LLC
Santa Barbara, California
Editorial Director: James Buckley Jr.
Designer: Patty Kelley
www.shorelinepublishing.com

Library of Congress Cataloging-in-Publication Data is on file with the publisher.

CONTENTS

KEY ICONS TO LOOK FOR:

Words to Understand: These words with their easy-to-understand definitions will increase the reader's understanding of the text, while building vocabulary skills.

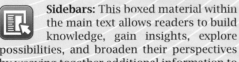

Sidebars: This boxed material within the main text allows readers to build knowledge, gain insights, explore possibilities, and broaden their perspectives by weaving together additional information to provide realistic and holistic perspectives.

Research Projects: Readers are pointed toward areas of further inquiry connected to each chapter. Suggestions are provided for projects that encourage deeper research and analysis.

Text-Dependent Questions: These questions send the reader back to the text for more careful attention to the evidence presented here.

Series Glossary of Key Terms: This back-of-the-book glossary contains terminology used throughout this series. Words found here increase the reader's ability to read and comprehend higher-level books and articles in this field.

INTRODUCTION

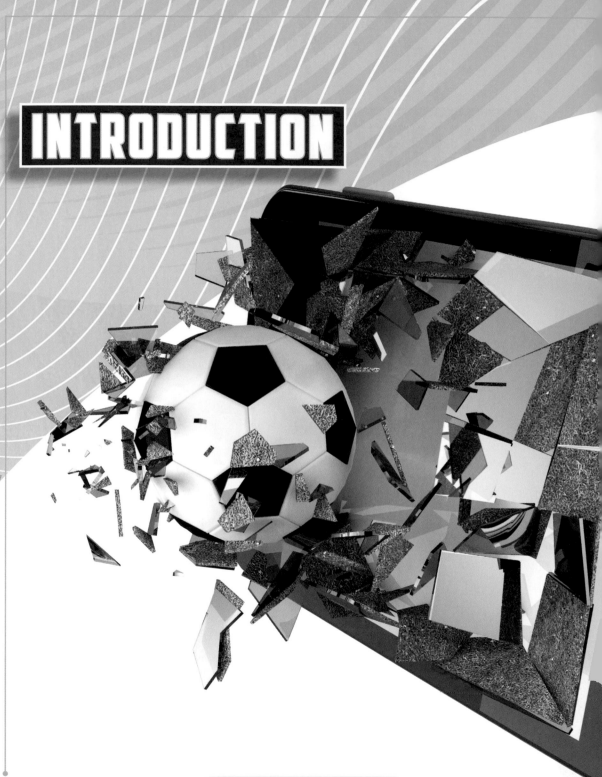

STEM IS THE HOTTEST BUZZWORD IN education. The letters stand for Science, Technology, Engineering, and Math. Those areas of study and work will be at the forefront of business, education, careers, and life for the coming decades. More jobs are opening up in those fields than in any other areas. But as this series shows, STEM is more than just programming computers or designing new mobile apps. The concepts of STEM cross over into just about every area of life. In this series, we focus on how STEM is impacting the world of sports.

This volume focuses on Technology. What is technology? It's a pretty broad area, actually. The definition is basically "using science for practical purposes." That is, turning the ideas of science into the reality of "things." In sports, that means new devices, new gear, new methods of training, and more. The goal for all of these STEM-related developments is to help athletes improve and help teams win. Sports fans benefit, too, as technology has made following and rooting for teams much easier and more involving.

CHAPTER 1

ATHLETES

TECHNOLOGY WON'T HIT A HOME RUN OR SCORE a touchdown. It won't set a world record in the Olympics or capture a World Cup. But the athletes who use their skills, hard work, training, and talent to do those things are turning more and more to technology to help them reach their goals.

Today's high-level athletes, unlike previous generations, grew up with tech. Many can barely remember a time without cell phones, so there is a comfort level that makes using tech in their sports lives easier. Today's athletes are as comfortable with digital gear as they are with their mitts, rackets, and skis. They've been using computers since they

From the field to the mat to the arena, athletes are more tuned in to tech than ever before.

were school kids (and some of them still *are* in school, of course: colleges are among the biggest tech users in sports). From studying video on iPads in the dugout or on the team bus, to watching computer models of their swings or their motion, athletes are calling on the tech they've grown up with to help them win. Meanwhile, scientists are giving these athletes a wide array of tools to improve performance and success.

There's an App for That

HANDHELD ELECTRONICS ARE ONE OF THE MOST VISible and popular uses of tech in sports. According to a Nielsen poll, more than 46 million Americans accessed fitness or health apps in 2014. Smartphones can be loaded with a wide variety of apps that do everything from count a runner's steps to show how far a soccer player has run during a game. There are literally hundreds of apps that can track data for athletes. Some are worn during exercise. The sensors in the smartphone record pace, heart rate, calories burned, duration, and other factors. Some apps can then provide a post-workout analysis so athletes can see how they are improving . . . or not! Such apps also keep track of ongoing workout data so athletes can compare their progress. Other apps guide athletes through workouts, either by audio or video "coaching."

WORDS TO UNDERSTAND

algorithm a series of instructions or code given to a computer to perform a task.

stamina a measurement of how long or hard a person can maintain an activity.

RoboWriter

We promise that a real human being wrote these words. But without that promise, you might not know. Several companies have created computer **algorithms** that can mimic human writing. One of the most popular uses for this technology is in sports. Because so much of sports reporting is numbers and stats, and because the language of a sport easily can be organized, programming a computer to create a sports story has never been simpler. Numerous small newspapers use products from companies such as Narrative Science to create sports reports. The fantasy sports leagues from CBSports.com deliver weekly updates to their baseball leagues, all written by a computer. The program takes in statistical results, merges them with one of the thousands of preprogrammed phrases, and what comes out is, usually, very much like what a human would write. Now journalists, like factory workers, have to worry that a robot might take their job!

Fitness bands worn on the wrist are the most visible evidence of this trend. The bands record data and beam it to the smartphone app to record and track progress. FitBit, Nike+Running, and My-FitnessPal are just some of the app-plus-band products being used by elite and weekend athletes alike. According to Nielsen, women make up the majority of the

An athlete can read information on a wrist screen that is beamed from the sensor strapped to his or her chest.

The smartphone apps link with wearable devices to provide athletes at all levels with information they can use.

people using these high-tech ways to keep in shape.

Are they working? Technology won't cut pounds or increase a person's **stamina**. Penn State professor David Conroy told NPR News, "One of the big challenges we're having now is how to make that data useful. We're drowning in data points without really capitalizing on them to change behavior more effectively."

In other words, all the apps in the world won't make you run, swim, jump, or sweat . . . until you, to borrow another phrase from sports, "just do it."

On Screen, on the Field

THE INSTANT AVAILABILITY OF DIGITAL VIDEO IS ONE of the most important developments in sports training in decades. Since its invention, film has been part of sports. Coaches were watching reel-to-reel tapes of their players and their opponents almost since the beginning of the movies. Videotape cassettes were routinely mailed among teams at the pro and college levels in major sports. Regular sessions were held in which a coach went over video with a team or individual players.

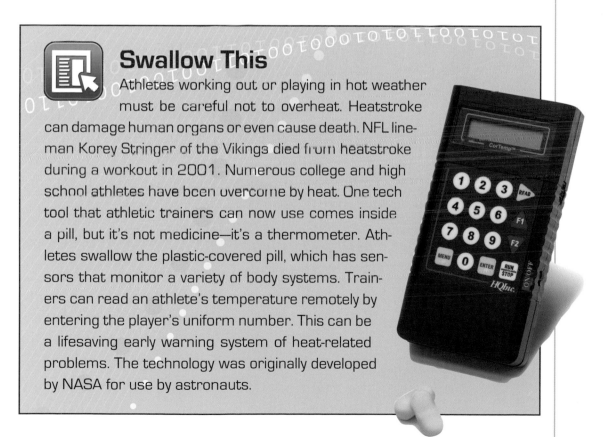

Swallow This

Athletes working out or playing in hot weather must be careful not to overheat. Heatstroke can damage human organs or even cause death. NFL lineman Korey Stringer of the Vikings died from heatstroke during a workout in 2001. Numerous college and high school athletes have been overcome by heat. One tech tool that athletic trainers can now use comes inside a pill, but it's not medicine—it's a thermometer. Athletes swallow the plastic-covered pill, which has sensors that monitor a variety of body systems. Trainers can read an athlete's temperature remotely by entering the player's uniform number. This can be a lifesaving early warning system of heat-related problems. The technology was originally developed by NASA for use by astronauts.

But there were drawbacks to all those systems, including the time needed to develop film, the need to do time-consuming editing to create relevant "highlight reels," and even the physical delivery time that could make a coach wait days.

Digital video and handheld devices have changed all that. Other than the sidelines of an NFL game (the league still bans tablet computers from the sidelines, and teams rely on old-time printouts of photos sometimes hand-carried down from the press box), tablets are part of every major pro and college team sport. A pitcher can return to the dugout to watch all the at-bats from a previous inning. A batter can watch every at-bat he has ever had against an upcoming pitcher. A basketball coach can show his team at halftime how they ran every play in the first half. The bus ride home from a college water polo game might include a "video" session with players each watching their own tablets.

Motion Studies

HOW DO YOU IMPROVE A GOLF SWING? HOW DOES a quarterback make sure he's passing in the most efficient way? How does a batter create a stance and swing that will lead to hits? Practice and coaching are, of course, the traditional way to study and improve any body movement in sports. The digital revolu-

tion has revealed another way that has been put to use in many sports environments: motion capture.

The idea of motion capture is to use high-resolution cameras and special sensors to film a person performing an athletic move. That move can then be broken down on the computer into tiny parts; it can also be manipulated by a coach or an athlete to find the perfect motion—or to spot flaws in the athlete's current motion.

The technology behind motion capture is similar to that used to create video games and some special effects in the movies. The

Sensors placed on the athlete's body create an animated form that matches the athlete's movements. That animation can then be studied and revised into a perfect form.

subject athlete has a set of electronic sensors strapped to his body at key points, including joints and key muscle groups. The camera recording the action highlights those sensors, creating a skeleton-like view of the person. That view can then be studied and examined by the athlete and the coach to look for ways to make the athlete better. Regular video is used, of course, but the motion capture's ability to cut the motion down to its key parts makes it more effective as a coaching tool.

Motion capture has been used in swimming with the help of underwater cameras. Tennis players and golfers can help tune their swing and also custom fit their rackets and clubs with "mocap," as it is sometimes called. And doctors even use it to test before-and-after motion of athletes recovering from injuries. If a picture is worth a thousand words, a motion capture image might turn into a thousand wins.

Social Connections

WHILE SPECIALIZED CAMERAS CAPTURE AN ATHletes' motion, social media helps capture the emotion of sports. In the early days of sports, the only way a fan could "hear" from a star athlete would be through the words of a newspaper. Even when books or articles were "by" a star, the words would usually come from a reporter. Radio began to let stars speak directly to fans, and TV made that even easier, but there was always a filter. There was always something something—a reporter, an announcer, an interviewer, a camera—between the player and the fan or the public.

Social media has changed all that. Players use the Internet, Twitter, Facebook, their own Web pages, and other avenues to reach directly to fans. In 2011, NBA superstar Shaquille O'Neal announced his retirement. He did not have a press conference where he stood before microphones and waited for questions. Instead, he posted a video on his Twitter feed. "Nineteen years, I want to thank you very much," he told his millions of followers around the world. "That's why I'm telling you first. I'm about to retire. Love you."

When an athlete gets in trouble, now his first move is to respond to criticism on his Twitter feed or on his or her Web site, not to wait for reporters to visit his house. It's a question of control: For decades, what an athlete said to the public was not always in his control. With social media, it is.

Athletes now have a direct and almost-instant way to connect with their fans, without the filter of the media.

Top Athletes on Twitter

The numbers go up and change all the time, but in recent years, these are the athletes with the highest number of followers on Twitter. For comparison, Ronaldo had more than 75 million followers in spring 2014.

- **Cristiano Ronaldo** (soccer)
- **Lionel Messi** (soccer)
- **Dwayne Johnson** (pro wrestling)
- **Kaka** (soccer)
- **LeBron James** (basketball)
- **Neymar** (soccer)

However, with that access comes its own set of risks. Athletes are human, often young, and don't always think before they tweet. Tech expert Charles Blair told *Forbes* Magazine, "In the old days, you had editors who could look at press releases. Now everything is off the cuff. There are no checks and balances."

In 2014, former New York Giants running back Derrick Ward was the latest in a line of athletes whose posts earned them bad press and criticism. He posted a note objecting to the on-screen kiss between Michael Sam and his boyfriend after Sam was drafted by the St. Louis Rams. Don Jones of the Miami Dolphins was fined for posting that the kiss was "horrible." Those types of posts were becoming outliers, however. Twitter has been around since 2006 and pro athletes, at least, are becoming much wiser about what they post. The vast majority now use their sites to post news of their accomplishments, praise for teammates or others, or positive opinions that can help their reputations.

TEXT-DEPENDENT QUESTIONS

1. What is the name of the technology that creates a point-by-point model of an athlete?
2. What condition does an internal thermometer seek to prevent?
3. What difficulty of the wearable tech revolution was mentioned in the chapter?

RESEARCH PROJECTS

Look at online listings of fitness apps. Which ones would be good for you to use in your life? What kinds of apps would help you meet your fitness goals?

CHAPTER 2

TEAMS & LEAGUES

ALONG WITH SUPPLYING TECH TO THEIR ATHletes, teams and leagues are turning to computers and machines to help them win, too. Coaches can now create digital playbooks that can be updated instantly. One click and every player has that weekend's game plan.

. . . and Bring Your iPad

Before the digital revolution swept over the sports world, NFL teams provided their players with the playbook in the form of a three-ring binder. It contained hundreds of pages of formations, diagrams, play names, position requirements, and much more.

Teams now provide coaches with tablets that can be instant teaching tools.

WORDS TO UNDERSTAND

formation in sports, the way a team lines up on the field.

telestrate "draw" on a computer screen to diagram something.

During training camp, when a player was told, "Coach wants to see you. And bring your playbook," he knew that he was being cut. The team wanted its book back. Today, a coach can erase the playbook from a player's iPad with the click of a button. Dozens of teams now provide tablets to their players that can be updated instantly over a network. Instead of photocopying dozens of sheets of paper, teams now distribute new plays or strategies to every player at once.

In summer 2012, for example, the Washington Redskins, passed out 125 iPads to their players, coaches, and staff members. The system has proved to be a winner with all concerned. "The players and coaches love the iPads. They can roam around, go from one meeting to another, and study the playbook and watch game video," Washington's director of information technology, Asheesh Kinra, told BizTech.com.

It's not just football, either. More than half of the teams in the National Hockey League use iPads regularly, even during games, according to SI.com. Coaches use them during timeouts and between periods to diagram plays or review action with players. One app is called iBench, which can help organize team videos. Other apps or programs let coaches draw on the screen to diagram new plays or **formations**.

"The ability to **telestrate** real-time on the iPad through the iBench app really allows us to not only show our players what is needed to succeed, but to teach our players how to succeed," Los Angeles Kings video coordinator Zach Ziegler told SI.com..

For the teams, it pays off in winning. For players who missed out on the revolution, the tech remains a dream.

"If I had all the data and all of that stuff back when I played football, the 1,500 catches that I had, over 20,000 yards, 208 touchdowns, I think I probably would have just doubled everything," Pro Football Hall of Fame receiver Jerry Rice said in 2013.

A coach uses a tablet to capture video of a Los Angeles Kings practice.

Making the Right Calls

THE EVER-IMPROVING WORLD OF VIDEO TECHNOLOGY has turned watching sports on TV into a series of timeouts. Most pro leagues now use some form of instant replay video to help on-court or on-field officials make sure they make the right call. The NFL has increased its use of instant replay every year since it first started experimenting with replay as far back as 1978. The current system has been in place since 1999, though it is constantly updated with new tech and new rules.

In 2014, Major League Baseball jumped in with both feet, creating a centralized system that umpires can use to review calls challenged by managers. The NBA lets officials look at courtside monitors to see if a three-point shot was taken "outside the arc," or if a shot was successfully attempted before time expired. The NHL uses replay on disputed goals. In the 2014 Stanley Cup playoffs, the eventual champion Los Angeles Kings were awarded a key goal in an early round game only after officials huddled around a monitor to make sure it was a legal shot.

Fans in general have supported the use of replay, as the bottom line for all parties is: Was that the right call? Critics believed that taking the "human element" out of sports— that is, the decisions by officials—was taking something away from the sport itself.

Step by Step

Here is the process that MLB began using in 2014 to use instant replay during games.

● After a play on the field, a team's manager can challenge the ruling of the umpire. (This does not include balls and strikes.)

● The umpiring crew then begins communication with a replay official at the league office in New York.

● The replay official looks at video of the action and determines if the call was correct or not.

● He gives that information to the umpires at the game, who then tell the two teams and the fans.

● The decision of the replay official cannot be reviewed.

Note: Each team starts with one challenge per game. If they make a successful challenge, they get one more challenge in that game. If they are not successful, they do not have any more chances to request video review.

Also, the umpire crew chief can ask for video review of a home run or foul ball call or any other call that he chooses.

Others worried that the games would slow down with endless replays of every play, call, score, or moment. However, as leagues have added and perfected different systems, most of that criticism has died away. Today, sports are looking for more and more ways to give officials video tools to make the right calls.

Goal-line technology used at the 2014 World Cup used seven cameras; (inset) if a goal was scored, it flashed on a screen worn by the referee.

Electronic Eyes

OFFICIALS USE MORE THAN VIDEO INSTANT REPLAY TO make sure that they make the right call. The use of multiple cameras and electronic "eyes" has made the split-second decisions by officials more accurate than ever.

In tennis, for example, the ball can move more than 100 miles per hour. Judging with the naked eye can be almost impossible, especially for shots that land on or near the side or end lines. Human judges are positioned to watch all of those, but since 2006, the pro tennis tour has added the Hawk-Eye system as a backup. Players or the head court official can request that a call be reviewed by the system. Operators call up a graphic representation of the shot. What results is an eerily accurate image of the "ball" as it hits the ground. Whether the ball hit the line or not is readily seen by players, officials, and fans—no more arguments.

Video is used to instantly create this animation. The black spot shows where the ball landed. This shot was "in"!

The Hawk-Eye system is also used in cricket to gather stats on where balls are hit, and even in snooker (a game similar to pool or billiards) to re-create the often-tricky shots that players make.

Soccer is the world's most popular sport, so with so many people watching, it's not surprising that tech has made an impact. The sport suffered through several controversies over officials' calls on whether a ball crossed the goal line or not. In the 2010 World Cup, England lost a goal when officials did not notice that the ball was clearly past the goal line. The outcry led to the rapid development of goal-line technology (GLT) for the 2014 World Cup in Brazil. Seven cameras were trained at each goal to cover every possible angle. After a goal or near-goal, the cameras instantly created a graphic to show where the ball went. If the on-field referees missed a call, they received a signal within seconds and could stop play to make the right call, thanks to GLT.

A key for all of these systems is speed. Sports depends on a rapid pace, and anything that impedes that pace is bad for fans and players alike. The ability of computers and cameras almost instantly to produce images for accurate judging has made this tech a vital part of many sports.

Watch What You Post

THE TECHNOLOGY OF SOCIAL MEDIA HAS CERTAINLY helped athletes connect with their fans (see page 16). But teams and schools are using the technology just as frequently, though with their own needs and aims in mind.

College athletic departments regularly monitor the social media posts of young people being recruited for their schools. And high school athletes need to watch what they

The use of Twitter and other social media by college athletes is carefully watched by schools.

post, too. The *Chicago Tribune* talked to several prominent recruiters in 2013. The interview subjects chose not to use their names in the article, but they all agreed that posting the wrong things can prevent a student from earning a scholarship. "We just decided this week to stop recruiting a handful of kids we really liked because of different things we saw on Twitter and Instagram," a recruiter from a Big Ten school told the *Tribune*.

A picture like this would just be embarrassing to post, but student athletes must beware of putting up images that can affect their careers.

Once a student is in college, the monitoring continues. A study by University of Maryland's Student Press Law Center found that more than 50 top universities have policies to monitor social media and keep an eye on their student-athletes. Some schools have policies in place that punish students for posting offensive or inappropriate information. Associate athletic director Felicia Martin of Texas Tech told the Maryland reporters, "We totally respect students' personal media presence. We respect that. We don't say: 'Don't have Twitter. Don't have Facebook. Don't do Instagram,' What we say is: 'Be responsible.'"

These policies can lead students into trouble. A football player at Lehigh University was suspended after he used racist words in a tweet. Numerous similar stories can be found in recent years. Other athletes got in trouble for posting pictures of themselves drinking or in places where they should not be.

However, the monitoring and punishment of what some might label free speech has raised concerns among some people. The issue of just how much right a school or a team has to control what a person posts or says is still being debated. As with everything in social media, it is very much a moving target, but one that will be part of the sports world for the future.

 ## TEXT-DEPENDENT QUESTIONS

1. What is the biggest reason that video instant replay can now be used in many sports?
2. Give three ways that teams are using video to help their athletes and coaches.
3. Schools monitor athlete's social media. Do you think that is right or wrong?

 ## RESEARCH PROJECTS

What's your favorite sport? Find some ways that your favorite sport could add even more tech. Think big; your idea could be groundbreaking!

Prudential Center
First Intermission
First Intermission
First Intermission
LEACH
33
PNC
BUD LIGHT
PLY PENALTY
0
PERIOD
1
1
8 SOG
16:47
SOG 14

CHAPTER 3

ARENAS, FIELDS, AND FANS

Modern scoreboards are packed with tech, from real-time scoring to video to moving screens.

ATHLETES TURN TO TECH TO IMPROVE THEIR skills. Teams and leagues use tech to make the games more fair. Arenas, stadiums, and fields are also packed with technology. Any stadium worth its popcorn has Wi-Fi for every fan, along with video scoreboards that provide crystal-clear replays and highlights. Fans in some stadiums have mini-monitors at their seats where they can choose video feeds, camera angles, or even play trivia games. Locker rooms at many modern arenas are wired to the teeth, with individual screens in each locker for players to study video (or play a video game). Any venue in which sports are played is now a hotbed of technology.

A Long Way from Fenway

ENWAY PARK IN BOSTON IS HOME TO MAJOR League Baseball's Red Sox. It's the oldest ballpark still in use in the Major Leagues. Its left-field scoreboard turns back the clock. Metals signs identifying scores and results from the innings—outs, run, hits, etc.—are hung from inside the left-field wall by a human operator. The dinged-up panels bear the scars of years of baseballs hitting them, along with paint faded by sun and rain. Such scoreboards are now just there for nostalgia. Today, massive high-tech scoreboards and video screens provide a treasure trove of information and entertainment to fans in the seats. Not only is this a benefit for fans, who can choose from numerous screens to watch and learn more about players and teams, but teams and stadiums can make big money selling ads on and around the screens.

The state of Texas has a famous slogan: "Everything's bigger in Texas." That goes for stadium video screens. Each new stadium in recent years seems to be trying to outdo one another for massive screen size. The 2012 debut of Cowboys Stadium in Dallas is a great example. The screen that hangs above the playing field is 160 feet wide and 71 feet tall, an area of nearly 12,000 square feet. Fans can see images on the screen almost instantly after each play. In between quarters and plays,

WORDS TO UNDERSTAND

grandstands a name for a large seating area at a stadium, usually long rows without any partitions.

scalper slang term for a person who illegally buys and sells tickets to an event, usually at a price above "face value."

highlight videos, commercials, announce-
ments, and more are shown on the enormous
screen. And it's all in high-definition video.

But by 2013, the Cowboys screen was in
second place. Houston's Reliant Stadium or-
dered a screen 52 feet tall and 277 feet wide.
The stadium claimed the scoreboard had the
largest screen in sports.

That distinction lasted for only a year. The
Texas Motor Speedway, home to NASCAR racing, built "Big Hoss TV" and claimed "world's
largest" status. The screen there, built over
racing **grandstands**, measures 218 x 94.6
feet. It's not as tall as Reliant's but it is 9,000

Like a lot of things
in Texas, the
"Big Hoss" video
screen is suppos-
edly the largest in
the world.

square feet larger in area. The owners of the stadium claimed to not only be aiming for the record, but also working to keep fans in the seats. With the increasing quality of home HD TV, sports owners worry that the in-home experience is becoming too good. By creating a way to enjoy both the HD quality of video and the in-person thrill of live action, places such as the Speedway hope to lure in more fans.

"The way to address [declining attendance] is by putting in a screen that, by comparison, is bigger than the ones you have at home, better than the ones you have at home, and you get the live feel, too," said Texas Motor Speedway president Eddie Gossage.

Look! Up in the sky! It's a flying camera! Well, not flying, but this wire-guided SkyCam gives TV viewers new and unique angles.

Cameras That Fly?

FANS OF THE NFL ARE USED TO SEEING ANGLES THAT normally only birds can see. Most NFL stadiums are equipped with wires strung throughout the stadium on which a "SkyCam" zooms above the field. An operator sends the camera zipping along the wires to follow the action, or to stay out of the way. Skycam has to be behind a kickoff, for instance, and can't be above the field during a punt. But by providing this birds-eye view, Skycam has really changed how fans see their favorite sport.

Handheld or worn on the body, the tiny GoPro cameras have helped capture amazing action sports video.

Next up in the air? Remote controlled flying cameras. Quadcopters equipped with video and still cameras are now used by hobbyists and professionals alike. Networks and teams are looking into ways to use these devices in their broadcasts.

GoPro cameras have made a big impact on extreme sports. The tiny boxes have been strapped to surfboards, skateboards, skydiving helmets, and much more. The camera's ability to record in wet, wild, or windy conditions, plus be controlled by the athlete himself, has created unprecedented visuals for fans and athletes alike.

Get Your Tickets Here!

FANS ENTERING A SPORTING EVENT NEED A TICKET, of course. Technology has radically changed how fans search for, buy, present, and even save tickets. Longtime fans fondly pull out cardboard ticket stubs from memorable games. The pieces of paper call back memories of great events, and can even be worth big money as memorabilia. A full ticket from a 1927 World Series game sold in 2014 for more than $41,000.

In the future, however, fans looking back on games in this era will not have, for the most part, ticket or ticket stubs. E-tickets are now standard for nearly all pro teams. Fans receive an email for them to print out a

The good old days: Many fans can boast of having a collection of ticket-stub memories, like these from the author's own treasure chest.

PDF with a unique bar code. The code is then scanned at the stadium gate. Some teams are able to scan from a smart phone, eliminating even the paper ticket.

In 2014, the Los Angeles Dodgers took the final step in this process. The team announced that it would no longer print and mail tickets to season-ticket holders. Instead, all such sales and deliveries would be electronic. Some longtime fans grumbled that they would miss the souvenir-ready cardboard. Other teams said that they would watch the experiment and see how it went.

This soccer stadium in Warsaw, Poland, even does away with human ticket takers. Fans just scan their tickets to open the moving gates.

The other big change in tickets is how they are sold on a secondary market. Fans are used to going to team Web sites to buy tickets, but what about tickets for sold-out events? Before the Web, buying a ticket to such an event often meant going to the event and wandering the parking lots and nearby streets, hoping to find a **"scalper."** Scalpers would often charge very high prices for what sometimes turned out to be counterfeit tickets. Such practices were also illegal for both buyer and seller. The online ticket resale market, made possible by the Web, printed PDFs, and scannable bar codes, has changed all that. Now sites such as StubHub offer a way for fans to buy legitimate tickets and to shop online for the best prices and seats. Pro leagues and teams are even partnering with StubHub and similar sites to help police against forgeries. In a change from the days when teams fought hard against ticket resale, today they are using technology to add to their bottom lines.

The Realities of Fantasy

TECHNOLOGY HAS TURNED FANTASY SPORTS INTO big business. The idea of fantasy sports is that fans create "teams" of their favorite athletes that then compete against other fans' teams in a wide variety of statistical competitions. Baseball was the first big fantasy sport, but it has been overtaken by fantasy

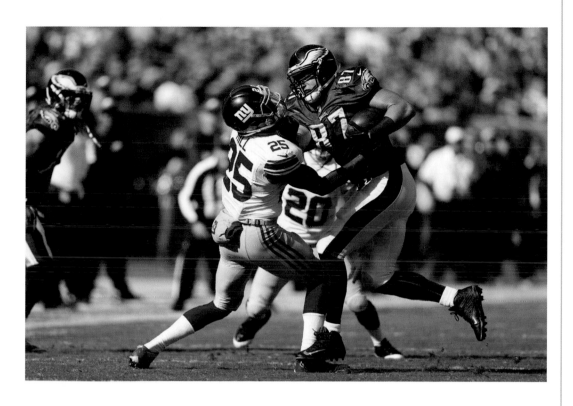

football. In 2014, more than 41 million fans played. Fantasy sports are also available for soccer, cricket, NASCAR, basketball, hockey, and much more.

The first fantasy players did all their own stats, reading newspaper box scores and calculating points weekly. With to-day's tech, however, fantasy is all-digital. Sites and apps send alerts to team "own-ers" with nearly every pitch, kick, or hit. Fans pay these sites to provide management for their leagues and teams, for scouting re-ports, and for seemingly endless sheets of stats for every situation. *Forbes* Magazine

This Philadelphia Eagles player has just made some fantasy player very happy.

Tech Drives Fantasy

NFL Media fantasy analyst Michael Fabiano is a familiar face on NFL Network and NFL.com, keeping fans up to date on the latest news for their favorite fantasy sport. Fabiano has been in the fantasy sports business for 15 years, and with the NFL since 2006. He commented on the impact of technology on fantasy:

"The biggest thing for fantasy was the dawn of the Internet. Before that, people just used paper and pen after Sunday's games to go through box scores and do stats for their teams. Now there are endless numbers of online services to run teams. Plus the growth in mobile apps, video on your phone, messaging, and more has helped fantasy sports grow enormously. We had NFL Now come out in the fall of 2014 as the next generation way for fans to connect with fantasy.

"Plus, the always-on presence of technology has changed the way people interact with sports. When I'm on my phone, I'm probably not talking to it. I run eight to ten teams, so I need to be aware of everything all the time. Mobile tech makes that possible.

"The technology in the future will focus on speed and information, because competition is a big part of this. People like to win, and faster access to news will help with that.

"The other big trend is that the 18-and-under group is the fastest growing segment of the fantasy sports population. People in high school in younger are going to have that as part of their lives. It changes the way you watch sports. Younger people are the ones who are going to make this even more popular, and the tech will be there for them to use."

called fantasy sports a multi-billion-dollar industry. Fans playing on sites that pay winners have made more than $100,000 a year in a few rare cases.

The impact of fantasy can also be seen on almost every sports broadcast. The running "crawl" along the bottom of ESPN or FOX Sports presents not just game scores, but individual player stats. Major sports leagues run their own fantasy games, which would have been unthinkable even two decades ago.

From in-stadium video to in-home ticketing, from cameras that capture reality to computers that track fantasy, technology has changed the game for fans.

TEXT-DEPENDENT QUESTIONS

1. What collectible will probably disappear thanks to scanning technology?
2. Where is the biggest video screen in the world?
3. How have computers put many illegal scalpers out of business?

RESEARCH PROJECTS

Cameras are invading every area of sports. Find clips online showing five different points of view of sports.

CHAPTER 4

GEAR

TECHNOLOGY HAS HAD A MAJOR IMPACT ON what players wear, use, throw, catch, and hit. An athlete from years gone by would hardly recognize the clothes that today's athletes wear, for instance. Using high-tech materials that are strong, lightweight, durable, and very stretchy, athletes today are cooler and safer than they've ever been. The protective gear they use also is packed with technology, along with advances in materials that provide added strength without added weight.

Nearly every sport can point to ways that new technology has aided gear that its athletes use.

This runner is packed with tech, though he still has to do the work.

What They Wear

SCIENCE AND TECHNOLOGY HAVE RADICALLY changed the look of sports. Synthetic fabrics have replaced cotton and wool in sports uniforms and clothing of all sorts. These fabrics are invented in labs, instead of being grown or "natural." It started with polyester and has grown to include Nylon, Spandex, Lycra, and a dozen other space-age materials.

● **Athletes get hot when they work out.** They sweat. A lot. With cotton or wool, the fabric absorbed the sweat. Clothes literally got heavier as an event went on. Plus, add the mud or rain they might play in. The synthetic materials helped solve some of that problem. In some cases, the fabrics repel moisture and thus don't get heavier. In other cases, the fabrics **wick**, or pull, the moisture away from the body, helping it evaporate more quickly and aiding cooling. European soccer players wear shirts made of sports wool, which combines some natural fibers with these sweat-wicking elements.

● **Athletes move.** A lot. They need clothing that is flexible and moves how their body moves. Wool and cotton were good, but not great. The addition of elastic strands made of rubber or synthetic elastics has made today's jerseys, pants, and other gear stretch easily, quickly, and comfortably.

WORDS TO UNDERSTAND

dimples on a golf ball, the tiny indentations that cover the surface

drag friction caused by air or water moving over a surface

wick a verb that means to pull away or separate

Though the LZR suit was outlawed, other companies, such as Jaked, make full-body suits that are legal to use in competition.

● **Athletes move through water.** Swimmers have the unique task of moving not through air, but through a liquid. Technology is on the case here, too. In 2008, a new type of full-body swimming outfit was created using materials and computer design. The suits reduced **drag**, or the friction of water over the body, more than 10 percent, which can be a lot at an elite level of competition. Together with world-class athletes, the LZR Racer suits literally changed the rule book—they were too good. "The thing that's really hurt more than anything else is the whole suit situation has devalued athleticism," swim coach David Salo told the *New York Times.* "A lot of kids who aren't in very good shape can put on one of these suits and be streamlined like seals." After more than 100 world records fell, swimming authorities ruled that the suits could not

This hockey gear worn by a modern player is more protective and also lighter weight than gear worn years ago.

be used in international competition. They felt that the suits were having more impact than the athletes and that fairness dictated that the swimmers return to older styles starting with the 2012 London Olympics.

● **Athletes get hit.** Physical sports such as football, lacrosse, and hockey provide players with pads and protection. Tech has helped make those materials lighter but still stronger. One of the most visible pieces of protective gear is the football helmet. While the effects of blows to the head are clearly negative, helmet designs are working to reduce that impact. Several companies invented sensors that can be put on or in helmets. These sensors measure the forces on the head and the helmet. The information can be read by a trainer or doctor on the sideline, who can quickly pull out a player. A California teenager invented a helmet that was said to be able to reduce concussions by 55 percent, though testing is still ongoing. The key for the success of these helmet technologies will be acceptance by players, who still resist most changes to the helmet.

Bouncing Into the Future

THE BALL IS THE BASIC PIECE OF GEAR FOR DOZens of sports. Technology has not forgotten about this most basic piece of equipment. Here are some examples.

At the 2014 World Cup of soccer, the teams used a ball that was the latest variation on an ever-changing design. Round balls are made of flat shapes that are sewn together to create a sphere. In 2006, the World Cup ball had 14 such panels. In 2010, it went down to eight. In 2014, there were six. The advantage? A ball

In-Vesting in Technology

Soccer players who took part in the 2014 World Cup took advantage of a pair of vest-related tech improvements.

The first kept them cool. With high temperatures and humidity in Brazil, site of the games, keeping cool was a priority. Teams were issued vests (right) made by adidas that were filled with ice. Nothing new there, but the materials the vests were made from kept the ice from freezing players' skin, while distributing the cooling over the player's trunk. Sleeves of the same material were also available.

The other vest was used by some teams in training. Players strapped on the bands and cords of a vest imbedded with sensors. Coaches could then track a player's movements, speed, and position using the sensors. A player could see a complete track of his path around the pitch. The teams could then arrange new tactics based on the movements tracked by the sensor vests, which also recorded a host of body measurements, including temperature and calorie loss.

with fewer seams and more flat area is more consistent in flight and easier to control.

Soccer balls can also now talk back. The miCoach "Smart Ball" from adidas has sensors built in to the ball. The sensors track the movement of the ball, as well as pressure put on it by players' kicks, and transmit the information to an app that can be read on a smartphone. A player can then see how fast his kicks went, what directions, and how he or she can improve his footwork to make the ball do exactly what he wants.

It's not just soccer. The 94Fifty basketball can act like a coach and a trainer. The ball's sensors count dribbles, bounces, spin, and motion and provide feedback after a workout. Users can read the arc angle on their shots, the force of their dribbles, and even their strength of dribbling with each hand.

Golf balls seem among the simplest balls in sports. Small, hard, covered with small **dimples**, they seem to all look the same. But millions of dollars of research and technology go into each company's design, inside and out of the ball. The number and arrangement of those dimples, for instance, is continually evolving as new tests show different flight paths. How the air moves over those tiny depressions helps determine how the ball flies through the air. By adjusting them through testing and computer modeling, experts can help players shoot straighter and farther. Of course, golf-ball makers want all these technological improvements to translate into sales of new golf balls.

OTHER GEAR

BEYOND THE BALL, SPORTS GEAR IS CONTINUALLY getting a high-tech workout. The Babolat tennis racket, for example, has sensors much like the miCoach soccer ball. Players using this racket can check the power or spin of their shots on their smartphone. "For the next generation of players, it will be a natural thing to switch your racket on before playing," said Babolat founder Eric Babolat. "I am really convinced that within a few years there will be no racquet that is not 'connected.'"

Golf clubs are computer designed and tested (see page 53) to incorporate designs that maximize control and minimize mishits. The shafts of the clubs are now often the same carbon fiber seen in bikes, cars, and other heavy-duty sports gear. They are not equipped with sensors yet, but it sounds like it's just a matter of time.

In cycling, the materials used to make the bikes are so lightweight that road racers have

Iron Byron and EARL

Robots are used to test sports gear to make sure that the equipment can handle the stress and heavy use that top athletes demand. One of the most well-known robot athletes is Iron Byron, once used by the PGA Tour to test golf clubs and golf balls. Named for legendary golfer Byron Nelson, the one-armed robot could hit thousands of golf shots exactly the same without ever tiring.

Bowling balls are tested by EARL (Enhanced Automated Robotic Launcher; above). The machine was also named for bowling great Earl Anthony. EARL can bowl left-handed or right-handed and can be programmed to create as many as 900 revolutions per minute on the ball. The United States Bowling Congress uses EARL to test new balls to make sure they follow national rules and to create a level playing field . . . or alley.

to meet a minimum weight for their bikes. The International Cycling Union puts that lower limit at 15 pounds (6.8 kg). The super-strong but super-light composite carbon fiber materials reduce the weight of the frame and gearing so much that the best bikes have gotten lighter and lighter. To create a level field for all teams, the UCI (the group's initials in French) put the minimum in place.

The bikes' composite materials use some of the high-impact product found in bulletproof vests or high-performance race cars. Woven strands of carbon and other materials condense to steel-like hardness but without the weight of the metal. To make their bikes reach the minimum, bike teams can add power-er meters that measure the rider's energy output as well as measure stresses on the bike, adding tech to an already tech-heavy machine.

Lightweight road bikes have helped cyclists increase speed and reduce time for long races.

Rolling Computers

EW SPORTS RELY AS HEAVILY ON TECHNOLOGY AS automobile racing. The drivers are still human (for now!), but the cars they race employ some of the most sophisticated tech in the sports world.

Formula 1 racing depends heavily on technology. The cars are all based on a single technical formula. Teams tinker constantly within that formula to find a better way for air to flow over the sleek cars. They try to coax more power from engines that are essentially the same for every team. The cars are made of very lightweight materials so that

"A modern Formula One car has almost as much in common with a jet fighter as it does with an ordinary road car. Aerodynamics have become key to success in the sport and teams spend tens of millions of dollars on research and development in the field each year."
—Formula 1.com

A Formula 1 steering wheel gives the driver a lot of ways to help run his car.

the engine has to move less weight. However, within those thin panels is a hardened steel cage that protects the driver. The outer shell actually is designed to break away on impact, which lets the energy of the impact lessen or dissipate before reaching the driver cage.

Much of the technology of these race cars is hidden from view, used in the design of the wings or the spoilers or the engine specs. However, fans can see the driver's steering wheel, and it is indeed more like a jet than a car. Formula 1 drivers have more than a dozen buttons they can push to operate various car systems, as well as several dials, gauges, and monitors. The wheel layout is designed to let a man moving 150 miles per hour maintain his concentration on the road while still being able to manipulate the computer and electronic functions of the car.

The stock cars of NASCAR are not as technical as Formula 1 machines, but tech still plays a huge part in the popular racing series. In the old days, racers kept track of their fuel use with a dial or a chalkboard. Today, computers take information beamed directly from the moving car and constantly adjust fuel readings to help teams know when it's time to make a pit stop. Today's hard-charging, step-on-the-gas drivers have to know as much about computer controls as about how to make a slingshot pass.

TEXT-DEPENDENT QUESTIONS
1. How did the design of the new World Cup ball help players?
2. What condition are new football helmet designs aiming to reduce or control?
3. How has tech helped cyclists ride faster?

RESEARCH PROJECTS
Time for a workout! Put on a wool sweater and jeans and run a mile or play some basketball. Then do the same thing in synthetic gear. Feel the difference? Can you take measurements of your temperature, time, or comfort level to compare playing in the two types of gear?

WINNING ... AND THE FUTURE

CHAPTER 5

THIS BOOK HAS PRESENTED NUMEROUS examples of ways that technology is making an impact in sports—from the gear players use to the places they play to the ways that fans enjoy the games.

Most would agree that technology has had a positive impact on sports. Players are safer and fans have many new ways to watch and cheer. The balls, clubs, rackets, and more can now be learning tools as well as sports gear.

But is all new technology good or useful? What about the issue of fairness? For instance, what about a high school in a wealthy area that can afford to get the latest and greatest gear, while a school in an area of lesser wealth cannot? If those teams play—and in many cities, they do—is that an even playing field? Also, think about how much the technology of sports is driven by money. Nearly all the tech in this book is made by companies for profit. They want to sell their gear not only to the pros, but to the weekend athletes. Do those companies always have the athletes in mind, or the bottom line? The research and innovations those companies do are important, and they have to make more money to do more research, but being aware of the reasons why technology is created also is important.

And what about the athletes themselves? Does all this technology provide too much aid to the athlete, taking away from his or her performance? Or are these developments just the latest in a century-long process to make

The next step beyond wearable tech is tattoo tech, such as this wire-packed electronic skin patch.

everything in life faster, easier, lighter, and more powerful?

All that said, what's next in sports and technology? The world of apps and digital video probably are the first place to look. Those are still evolving technologies. As more and more people turn to them, more and newer ways to help those people will emerge. Size is another area to look at. Digital gear used by athletes needs to avoid getting in their way or weighing them down. Designers and engineers will continue to shrink what they make. Look for more and more advances in "wearable tech," both inside and outside the sports world.

One idea under study is a tattoo that can conduct electricity. Put on the skin under superstrong glue, the tiny wires and sensors can gather and transmit information about the wearer. In the future, the tattoos might work together with other devices, such as smartphones or other monitors.

On the pro sports field, the use of tech to gather the "big data" that is changing almost every area of human life will increase. Sports have always been packed with stats and numbers. The ability of computers to gather, analyze, and draw conclusions from huge sets of numbers will continue to grow in impact. A quick example from sports: In 2014, more Major League defenses shifted their alignments radically than in any previous season. The reason? Teams now have several seasons of data from which to draw up these new ways to defend individual hitters. Did technology prevent your favorite team from getting a hit in the last game . . . or did it save the day and make your team a winner?

Win or lose, technology will be part of the game more and more in the coming years.

FURTHER RESOURCES

Books
Bicycle Technology
By Rob van der Plas and Stuart Baird
Van der Plas Cycle Publishing, 2010

Fitness Tech: Get Fit and Healthy Using Cutting-Edge Wearable Technology
By Don Fitch
Well-Being Skills, 2013
(Note: Available as Kindle e-book)

Official BBC Sports Guide: Formula One 2014
By Bruce Jones
Carlton Books, 2014

Technology in Football
By Shane Frederick
Sports Illustrated for Kids, 2013
(also similar titles on baseball, basketball, and hockey)

Sports Technology
By Stewart Ross
New Apple Media, 2012

Web Sites
Sportstechie.com
From the World Cup to the NBA, from the NFL to MLB, this site tracks and updates news on how technology of all kinds is impacting the world of sports. Search by sport or athlete or visit their news section for details on new apps.

popularmechanics.com/outdoors/sports/
Popular Mechanics, one of the world's best magazines for hands-on science, has a section of its site devoted to sports technology. Original articles and links to the magazine give you information on different sports, new gear, and new ways to link tech and sports.

SERIES GLOSSARY: WORDS TO UNDERSTAND

aerodynamic The science of how air moves and how objects move through it

applications In this case, ways of using information in a specific way to find answers

carbon fiber A material woven of carbon atoms that offers a wide range of high-strength and high-flexibility properties

cognitive training Software and hardware that trains the brain and the body's senses

fluid dynamics The science of how air or liquid moves over a surface

GPS: Global Positioning System Technology that bounces a signal off satellites to pinpoint the exact location of where the signal originated from

logistics the science of organizing large numbers of people, materials, or events

parabola a symmetrical curved path. In stadiums, a roof overhang can create a parabola by bouncing noise from below back down toward the field of play

prosthetics devices that replace a missing human limb

prototype a model of a future product made to test design and engineering issues

rehabilitation the process of returning to full physical ability through exercise

velocity measurement of the speed of an object

ventilation the easy movement of air around or within a body or a system

INDEX

Photo Credits

About the Author

James Buckley Jr. has written more than 100 books on sports for young readers. He is a former editorial projects manager for *Sports Illustrated* and a senior editor at NFL Publishing, where he was on the team that started NFL.com. In 2012, he was the editor of *NFL Magazine.* His recent books include titles on baseball history, the Pro Football Hall of Fame, and even robots, along with biographies of Jesse Owens, Muhammad Ali, and Roberto Clemente. He is president of Shoreline Publishing Group and lives in Santa Barbara, California.